Selected Anonymous Marginalia

Selected Anonymous Marginalia ♡

VOLUMES I–III

EDITED BY Liam Agrani

life-
form
books

Selections from "Volume I" were first published in 2010
as *Volume One* by Beard of Bees Press (chapbook number 58).
The complete "Volume I" was subsequently published in 2010
as *VOLUME ONE (Selected Anonymous Marginalia)* by BlazeVOX Books.

Life-Form Books | WWW.LIFEFORMBOOKS.ORG
Post Office Box 29575, Providence, Rhode Island 02909

FIRST EDITION

ISBN 978-0-692-13510-5

Contents

VOLUME I   *1*

VOLUME II   *77*

VOLUME III   *145*

l and fals vanegloir,
onfusioun,   475
 worschip thairfoir,
land up and doun,
aw he maid him boun.
d crawin ane note,
nt him be the throte.   480

ie with him hyit,
ot lytill dout.
k and Toppok cryit;
th ane cry come out;
: and gaif ane schout: 485
-with ane hiddeous beir—
l Chantecleir!'

mony yell and cry,
r breist can beit;
 ane extasy,   490
ning and in sweit.
s left thair meit,
 lyand thus in swoun,
atioun.

In Chaucer there is a great animal chase at this point

VOLUME I

TRANSCRIPTION OF SELECTED MARGINALIA FOUND IN
A COPY OF *GREEK LYRIC POETRY* PUBLISHED IN 1993
BY OXFORD UNIVERSITY PRESS

p. 9   speaks of
        being scared
        earlier

        shows several
        sides of
        personality

p. 31   adv. to
        those that
        respect do
        measure

p. 42   old age
        will
        catch up
        to
        everyone

p. 53   don't accept
        tyranny

TRANSCRIPTION OF SELECTED MARGINALIA FOUND IN
A COPY OF *GERARD MANLEY HOPKINS: POEMS AND PROSE*
EDITED BY W. H. GARDNER AND PUBLISHED IN 1970
BY PENGUIN BOOKS, LTD.

p. 27   white
        birches

        feathers

p. 28   pussy willows

p. 31   his soul in his body

p. 32   the body will rest on the soul as the
        shadow of a rainbow on a meadow

p. 6   the salesman
or the farmer's
daughter?

p. 7   hope —

illusion
v.
reality

p. 8   not
unpleasant

p. 17   doesn't know what to expect

p. 46   instinct

p. 176   sells
his
soul

p. 206   seems
strange
the cause
didn't
think of

his
married
state
before

p. 208   how
intimate

p. 210   alone

p. 227   framed
by
chance

p. 238   unconsciousness

p. 239   definition of mind

p. 252   man's
aloneness

p. 262   aloneness

p. 269   ah, if only she could
be an actress

p. 271   **21**

p. 277   obvious

p. 279   always the
          "if" sentences

p. 300   paralysis of the will

p. 329   the
          tragic
          view

p. 374   alone

p. 378   another
          "if"
          that
          failed

TRANSCRIPTION OF SELECTED MARGINALIA FOUND IN
A COPY OF *THE RISE OF SILAS LAPHAM* BY WILLIAM DEAN
HOWELLS, PUBLISHED BY SIGNET IN 1980 AND PREVIOUSLY
OWNED BY JEAN CAROL CUSCIO

p. 9 mother

p. 16 wife

nature

p. 20 looked at

p. 21 a made thing
self-conscious

p. 26 the daughter

p. 29 light

p. 30 their social dilemma

p. 42 nature

p. 44 quiet/morality

p. 46 marriage

p. 49 myth

p. 57 $

p. 62   what traveling can do

p. 63   ha!

p. 68   nature

p. 75   there was an accident
         on his boat once

p. 82   self-consciousness

p. 86   superstitious

p. 88   superstitious

p. 107   idleness

p. 120   ha!

p. 123   passive

p. 161   like a play

p. 169   fashion

p. 170   ha!

p. 171   etiquette

p. 175   ha!

p. 193   oh!

p. 203　**wow!**

TRANSCRIPTION OF MARGINALAIA FOUND IN A 1963
COPY OF ROBERT HENRYSON'S *POEMS*, PUBLISHED BY
OXFORD UNIVERSITY PRESS AND FORMERLY OWNED
BY JOHN COLLINS

p. 2   Nonsense

        You know you're in for human
        degradation, perversion through ignorance's
        human perversity.

p. 4   waxes, lyric,
        carried away
        by his own
        logic.

p. 5   science
        likened
        learn
        gets nervous

p. 7   arm in arm
        pilferers
        manner
        womb
        stomach

p. 10   again, negative humor

p. 11   the extra dishes
        bring on trouble

p. 13   lusty?

sexy?

courageous?

proud?

p. 15   In Chaucer there
is a great animal
chase at this point

p. 16   No great
lover is ever
jealous

who

p. 90   dismal
full of care

caused
to fall

p. 91   sexual desire

p. 93   in haste
outcast

p. 94   oh Blasphemy!

p. 95   like a bully

p. 96   down
        shows off
        hope vs. despair
        one eye laughs
        one weeps

        to comb your golden hair
        a sign of idleness

p. 97   the moon closest
        to the earth is the
        most fickle of
        planets.

TRANSCRIPTION OF SELECTED MARGINALIA FOUND IN
A COPY OF *THE POEMS OF JOHN MILTON* PUBLISHED IN 1953
BY THE RONALD PRESS

p. 35   river on which
         Cambridge is
         located

p. 39   a lush
         poem

         in love
         with Spring—
         a riot of
         imagery—

p. 82   liquid
         notes

p. 87   (the thoughtful one)

p. 113   almost
         swamped
         by the
         beauty
         of
         goodness

p. 205   2 death

         1 apple

p. 208   his mistake
is that he was the
aggressor, not God—

p. 210   what if ever
now we are
doing the will
of God?

p. 214   dead

scattered

useless

p. 218   angelic
physiology

p. 223   brighter
and
more
definite

p. 227   wonder

p. 237   the least
directed of
the spirits

p. 238   he
doesn't
even

recognize
what
we have
lost—

p. 241 to get
even with
God

p. 260 sacred influence
of light

p. 267 Justice:
getting exactly
what one
deserves; no
less, but
certainly no
more

Mercy: getting
more than
one deserves

p. 299 like symphony, an
epic is composed
of movements
which balance +
interact with
one another

Heaven
Hell
Earth

p. 301   Spring Flowers

p. 302   [beautiful +
         doomed]

p. 357   Invocation
         again

p. 389   the obj. of this
         poem is to
         justify the
         ways of God
         to man

         who is
         warned

p. 30   promise
of
grace which
saves repentant
nature

p. 31   All world
quiet

stars &
sun

p. 32   music
symbol
of harmony
in nature
+ universe

moon's
sphere

figures
of heaven

p. 68   nature
         mourning
         loss

         nymphs

p. 69   conflict of poetry

         +

         reality

         digression

         wonder at value
         of long preparation
         for poet's trade

         combined idea of
         fates

p. 70   shepard

p. 71   2nd digression

         pastor as
         shepard +
         sheep congregation

p. 78   builds
         rushing
         passion

p. 79   idolatry

p. 82   books have
a life

p. 85   evil can
be learned
other ways
than from
reading

TRANSCRIPTION OF THE MARGINALIA FOUND IN THE
"PARADISE LOST" SECTION OF THE *SELECTED WORKS
OF MILTON* EDITED BY MAYNARD MACK AND PUBLISHED
IN 1950 BY PRENTICE HALL

p. 137   who should
          go to earth?

p. 139   man not in
          harmony with each
          other

p. 143   epic simile
          based on
          nature

p. 144   the other
          shape was like
          a shadow

p. 149   chaos is
          complaining about
          losing kingdom

p. 151   but a cloud
          saves him

p. 152   ?

TRANSCRIPTION OF MARGINALAIA FOUND IN
A 1966 COPY OF JOHN LYGATE'S *POEMS*, PUBLISHED
BY OXFORD UNIVERSITY PRESS AND PREVIOUSLY
OWNED BY JOHN COLLINS

p. 50   dark blue

         holly + woodbine =

         constancy?

p. 51   feverish
         love sickness
         uninhibited
         dismayed

p. 59   lies

p. 71   the force that keeps
         the lover from the
         lady.

p. 73   As soon as
         you mention a lady, you must go into a bravura
         performance, beginning w/ the disclaimer that you
         can't describe her.

COMPLETE TRANSCRIPTION OF MARGINALIA FOUND IN
J.'S COPY OF *SHORT WALKS IN CONNECTICUT* PUBLISHED
BY THE PEQUAT PRESS, 1968

p. 68   June 15 – July 15

p. 70   overlooks silica quarry

p. 72   passes cedar swamp + Ind. res.

p. 74   ½ mile to a lovely
picnic area with view

TRANSCRIPTION OF MARGINALIA FOUND ON THE COVER
OF A 1962 PRINTING OF SAMUEL TAYLOR COLERIDGE'S
BIOGRAPHIA LITERARIA, FROM EVERYMAN'S LIBRARY

in big
in side

use
story as
part of image
technique in story form

TRANSCRIPTION OF THE MARGINALIA FOUND IN A COPY OF
LESS THAN ONE, THE SELECTED ESSAYS OF JOSPEH BRODSKY,
PUBLISHED BY FSG IN 1986 AND PURCHASED IN A USED
BOOKSTORE IN MASSACHUSETTS

p. 7   The reason for lying
was motivated by a social
Standard
at that
time,
Therefore
it implies
that
existence
really
shapes
consciousness

p. 17   His
point
of view

p. 18   repeats the condition of

the
landscape
the
building
the
system
look the

same,
therefore, it
conditioned him
to see life as

p. 23 it is confused, but somehow
brings you closer to him
since it is the human
nature and through writing
he discov.

TRANSCRIPTION OF MARGINALIA FOUND IN
CYRIL CONNOLLY: JOURNAL AND MEMOIR PUBLISHED
BY TICKNOR & FIELDS IN NEW YORK IN 1984 AND FOUND
WITH THE FICTION AT J. M.'S HOUSE

p. 1   modest, elegant

p. 34   Mrs. Wilkes' distress at her portrait

p. 35   1904–1974

p. 37   "to write rather well about
many things"

p. 41   C.'s "homosexuality"—
the mistake

p. 111   on his qualities as a reviewer

p. 112   a fact about an essay needed in
The Selected Essays

p. 114   on hedonism

p. 153   the epitaph

p. 176   C. on sex is painful.
impossible—

p. 199   advice to a reviewer

p. 205   parody

p. 212   wonderful story about
          Jean. The future wife + Paris
          in the 20's

p. 218   Lesbian questionnaire

p. 222   depression at being in England

p. 254   famous encounter w/
          V. Woolf—nobody can
          outdo the English in this

p. 269   perils of authorship

p. 287   end of marriage
          to Jean

p. 296   wonderful
          fantasy monologue

TRANSCRIPTION OF SELECTED MARGINALIA FOUND IN
A 1984 COPY OF HENRY JAMES'S *PORTRAIT OF A LADY*
PUBLISHED BY PENGUIN CLASSICS

p. 68   like a garment?

p. 74   clothes

p. 98   clothes

p. 102   "suffering"

bad pastime

p. 278   picture

p. 325   deceit

p. 352   me

p. 398   me

323

untruths

p. 470   like a painting

p. 596   pic.

p. 619   ha!

p. 635   "the kiss"

TRANSCRIPTION OF SELECTED MARGINALIA FOUND IN
A COPY OF FRANZ KAFKA'S *THE TRIAL* (TRANSLATION BY
BREON MITCHELL) PUBLISHED BY SHOCKEN IN 1998

p. 68   of the
law court
offices in
the attic

p. 74   poisoned air
in the court

p. 82   one court job – flogger

p. 140   painter in attic

p. 146   court = vanity

court = hunt

p. 148   lack of
air in painter's
place

[inside front cover]

Write an essay exploring the underlying
meaning of the weird relationship between
Huld and Block

[title page]

Now the school thinks Sarah Clark was the 3rd person last night
they want to drug test all of them   Sarah should go to Shauna and tell
her that she should confess because if Sarah is tested well you know

[back cover]

I'm really surprised Shauna
didn't do this. She thinks
she has a really
good voice

p. 2   does not
take action

p. 4   he is
insulted
he is acting
strange

p. 5   he thinks
that his friends
are joking
with him they
don't really
care

p. 6   in society
this is
the concept
of the
book

the guilty
people stand
out in the
crowd

he stood out

p. 89   they
        were
        expecting
        him

p. 98   thinks he
        deserves
        better

p. 120 even
        more
        absurd

p. 121 don't
        argue
        you will
        make it
        worse for
        you
        this is
        all advice
        given by
        his lawyer
        the lawyer is
        telling him
        how to win
        the case
        by laying
        low. Best
        advice yet
        but he
        thinks it is absurd

p. 125   K has
some
nerve

p. 170   the 2 of
them
laughing
at
K.

p. 173   you will
be like me
if you spend
all of your
time trying
to get off

p. 203   foreshadow

p. 204   metaphorical
darkness

p. 206   K. feels
superior
again

p. 220   if he
accepted
him being
guilty
whether he
was or wasn't
there would be no problems

p. 221 totally
incapable
of any
decisions
in his
life

p. 225 seeing
her puts
everything
into
perspective

COMPLETE TRANSCRIPTION OF MARGINALIA FOUND IN A
COPY OF *SIDHARTHA* BY HERMAN HESSE PUBLISHED IN 1952
BY NEW DIRECTIONS AND OWNED BY THE STONINGTON
HIGH SCHOOL LIBRARY, PAWCATUCK, CT (LAST TAKEN OUT
BY AMANDA KENYON IN SEPTEMBER OF 1997)

p. 23   contradicts
         himself
         knows
         everything
         no
         self
         love?

p. 62   self love?

p. 67   has
         everything—

         pleasure
         garden

p. 68   what makes
         others happy doesn't
         please him

p. 70   forebode

p. 76   love

TRANSCRIPTION OF SELECTED MARGINALIA FOUND IN A
COPY OF GEORGE GISSING'S *THE ODD WOMAN* PUBLISHED
BY W. W. NORTON AND CO. IN 1977

p. 36   R.
         introduces
         M. to the
         typewriter

p. 37   How dismal!

TRANSCRIPTION OF MARGINALIA FOUND IN A COPY
OF *THE SELECTED POEMS OF JOHN GAY* PUBLISHED
BY CARCANET IN 1979

p. 33   you deserve to be
beaten over your
head for singing
so bad

out of realm
of art into real
world

COMPLETE TRANSCRIPTION OF MARGINALAIA IN
A COPY OF *THE VARIETIES OF RELIGIOUS EXPERIENCE*
BY WILLIAM JAMES, PUBLISHED IN 1914 BY
LONGMANS, GREEN AND CO. AND PRESENTLY
OWNED BY A SMALL LIBRARY IN CONNECTICUT

p. 171   **Look up**
          St.
          Augustine
          in N.T.

TRANSCRIPTION OF SELECTED MARGINALIA FOUND IN A
COPY OF JANE VAN LAWICK-GOODALL'S *IN THE SHADOW OF
MAN* PUBLISHED IN 1971 BY HOUGHTON MIFFLIN

p. 49   meat eating

p. 52   tool
          making

p. 95   learn
          ing

p. 135   jealousy

p. 163   play

p. 170   they were gentle

p. 249   Next Page!

p. 250   read this

[inside cover]

In what way is Virgil's Aneid an
expression of the history and ideals
of the Augustan Age.

p. 1   alacrity

p. 30   s
        t
        o
        r
        m

p. 49   b
        a
        n
        q
        u
        e
        t

p. 58   t
        r
        o
        j
        a
        n

h
o
r
s
e

p. 156 river
styx

TRANSCRIPTION OF SELECTED MARGINALIA FOUND IN
A COPY OF DANTE'S *INFERNO* (TRANS. JOHN CIARDI)
PUBLISHED IN 1954 BY THE NEW AMERICAN LIBRARY

p. 28   narrative is recalled

p. 29   eater

p. 31   the
         moral
         death

p. 37   Instrument of grace, elevation of beauty

p. 60   embarrassment
         of oneself

p. 81   radical
         evil

p. 109   sex

         $

p. 127   unnatural

p. 131   original sin

p. 210   Bad news
         for
         Dante

p. 223   tongue
         of
         flame

COMPLETE TRANSCRIPTION OF THE MARGINALIA
FOUND IN A 1975 EDITION OF *HOW TO DO THINGS
WITH WORDS* BY J. L. AUSTIN (FOUND IN A WESTERN
MASSACHUSETTS BOOKSTORE)

p. 35   Caligula

TRANSCRIPTION OF SELECTED MARGINALIA FOUND IN
A COPY OF DONALD BARTHELME'S *SNOW WHITE* PUBLISHED
IN 1972 BY ANTHENEUM AND PREVIOUSLY OWNED
BY ANDRE A. SACKNER

p. 56   solidarity

hermit

alone

anti-social

p. 75   Fuck you
if you never agree to
the ruin
why damn it
do you contribute
100% to it?

p. 77   Waiting
for Godot

p. 82   It's good like it is

the hysteria already

shit—do we have problems
we don't even know what they are
we are confused. Snow White is absurd.
She doesn't know it. She's hoping.

Cynicism. Sarcasm
helps to keep sanity
maybe.

p. 83 Not
yet

What?

Don't be silly

All 3 + more

As many as their
bodies can handle, individual
preference

present is plenty to work with

Also—don't mock
your readers they
support you financially
if nothing
else.

I scratch that   He is not mocking his readers
but rather asking them to play

p. 107 Use of these
phrases brings them to a lite
not yet seen before.

How absurd
they are.

p. 132 Oh Snow
White
help me not
be you
by showing me
your
absurdity

p. 170 Because there
is no other
purple
blood
around
for the
moment

TRANSCRIPTION OF SELECTED MARGINALIA FOUND
IN A COPY OF VIRGINIA WOOLF'S *TO THE LIGHTHOUSE*
PUBLISHED BY HARCOURT BRACE AND OWNED FOR SOME
TIME BY A STUDENT AT ST. JOHN'S UNIVERSITY

p. 10   lang

codes

Oedipus complex

p. 15   distinctions?

p. 23   marks—protections

p. 26   own words?

p. 28   a feeling of being trapped?

p. 29   trapped on canvas

p. 32   use quote about
the "I"

p. 34   a woman's power vs. a man's
power to
control?

p. 41   framed

thought
process

frame

p. 53   interactions
way to look at it

p. 55   limits

the realization of one's limits?

p. 60   a
lover's
bloom

p. 61   belatedness?

p. 65   the self turning in
on itself

p. 81   male / female ways to preserve the world

p. 91   time

secret

p. 92   belatedness

b/c her
children
will never
be as happy
as they
are now, and

they, too,
like her,
will realize
this too
late?

p. 98   sep. spheres

Mrs. Ram:
in touch
w/
life

Mr. Ram
in touch
w/
ideas

p. 106   absence

p. 126   grandma?

p. 128   merge

p. 129   absence

p. 136   lang — a way to
order
reality

p. 138   silent lang.?

p. 141   emptiness

p. 179   lang.

p. 185   me
                 +
                 Andy

p. 203   Panic
                 + emptiness

p. 219   the infinite?

p. 267   Like Mr. R. to Mrs. R.

TRANSCRIPTION OF SELECTED MARGINALIA FOUND IN
A COPY OF PLATO'S *TIMAEUS* PUBLISHED BY THE LIBRARY
OF LIBERAL ARTS IN 1959 AND PREVIOUSLY OWNED
BY BOB COOPERRIDA

p. 17   words
         of the
         account
         will be
         unchanging

p. 18   purpose of sight

p. 22   fire, earth, air, water

p. 50   it continually changes into
         shape

p. 52   to declare emphatically

p. 53   form

         particular

p. 45   ie: ragged
         images

p. 65   var
         of air

p. 74   sight +
         hearing

p. 75 pain is
a violent
change of
the normal
state

TRANSCRIPTION OF SELECTED MARGINALIA IN A COPY
OF PLATO'S *PHAEDO* (FROM THE *COLLECTED PLATO*,
PUBLISHED BY BOLLINGEN, 1961) AND BELONGING TO THE
STONINGTON PUBLIC LIBRARY, STONINGTON, CT

p.43   law of
compensation

p.44   hence
position
painting

p.46   heaven
+
hell

p.47   #1

p.48   condemnation
of poets!

p.50   attitude
depends
upon
belief

p.52   heaven
+
hell

p.55   recollection

p. 59   recollection

p. 62   weak

p. 63   but what
         about
         persuasion?

p. 67   birds

p. 68   musical
         analogy

p. 80   2 levels
         of reality

p. 86   numbers

p. 88   2

p. 89   ie. poetry
         ie. condemna
         tion of poet
         — Homer as
         education of
         Greece —
         — purgatory —

         the road
         to Hell is paved
         w/ good intentions

p. 93   re. Oceaners

TRANSCRIPTION OF SELECTED MARGINALIA FOUND
IN A COPY OF THE 1973 OXFORD EDITION OF
SIR PHILIP SIDNEY'S *POEMS*, PREVIOUSLY OWNED
BY SAMANTHA STEAD

p. 117   love at first sight

p. 118   ways of ornamenting love poetry

p. 119   yet—but/still

p. 120   pure, dazzling

p. 121   touchstone/touch paper

p. 123   illuminate

p. 125   secular nature
          for love

p. 128   jealousy, selfish lust

p. 132   ungratefulness is virtue

p. 133   trying to reassure self

p. 135   clever twists

p. 140   heavy caesura

p. 145   pleasurable experience

p. 147   earthly love blind
spiritual platonic
love — sighted

p. 152   get better

p. 155   reject idea
of poetic
inspiration

p. 156   progress + day

p. 172   breakdown

p. 175   complete reversal of
normal relationships

p. 181   moon trying to comfort him for
loss of sun

p. 188   inconclusive

A COMPLETE TRANSCRIPTION OF THE MARGINALAIA
FOUND IN A COPY OF *THE SELECTED EPIGRAMS OF MARTIAL*,
PUBLISHED IN 1963 BY INDIANA UNIVERSITY PRESS AND
PREVIOUSLY OWNED BY ALLISON M. SCOTT

p. 33   Thomas Brown, 1663 – 1704

I do not love thee, Dr. Fell
The reason why I cannot tell
But this I know, and know thee well
I do not like thee, Dr. Fell

cannot rationalize
the emotional basis
for relationships

p. 35   English direct
and savage

Latin elegant
and corrosive

p. 42   padding

p. 44   California

or

New York

praise

p. 46   miniature
mock
epic

p. 50   existential
statement

the
nowhere
niche

cf.
Trimalchis

p. 54   possessing

p. 95   no doubt
you've been
rejected

p. 105   incestuous,
sordid

p. 109   marriage of
homosexuals

p. 111   long poem to
explain why
he doesn't deserve
an epigram

TRANSCRIPTION OF SELECTED MARGINALIA FROM
A COPY OF THE COLLECTED WORKS OF GOETHE PUBLISHED
IN STUTTGART IN 1881, PURCHASED BY A MR. SPALDING
OF 92 NORTH MIDDLE (IN 1893), AND FOUND BY
MY MOTHER'S FRIEND MARGARET ELLEN

p. 2   May 8 1784
        on a journey to the
        mtns.

p. 21   the game de-
        scribed in a
        letter

p. 36   Spring over (all through) the whole year

p. 44   Frankfurt   1768 or 9

p. 52   printed same year

p. 55   one of most notable early poems

p. 56   untranslatable
        of Venus and
        Adonis.

        rapture

p. 58   valor of blossoms

p. 60   Thursday June 15 '75

p. 61   Same time
on the shore
of the lake

p. 80   permanence in the middle of change

p. 122   Sept 4, 1797

p. 136   May or July

p. 139   June

p. 157   June 1st, 1781
sent to France

finish straw-
berries of season

p. 174   May 1798

p. 178   May 1797

p. 236   anniversary of
building of

printed 1815

p. 239   what you are doing on any
given day only the next day can
tell you

p. 247 of Pindar
of
The Psalms

p. 250 15 Sept. 1780

p. 256 flowering feel

Graces

Bacchus

p. 258 Keats "Nightingale"

p. 260 Love would make
der Taube har
der

p. 263 at intervals

p. 264 mentioned in letter

p. 285 sign of
Goethe's re-

nature

p. 287 19th Aug 1823

TRANSCRIPTION OF SELECTED MARGINALIA FOUND IN A
COPY OF THE 1995 PRENTICE HALL EDITION OF *THE VISUAL
ARTS: A HISTORY* BY HUGH HONOUR & JOHN FLEMING

p. i   "All that is solid melts into air"
       Karl Marx

p. 96   gesture
       of
       extreme grief
       bodies
       are reduced
       to shapes
       analyzed

p. 101   slight rotation of hand

p. 102   silhouette

p. 114   confident pose of man

p. 121   – detail

       – psychology

       – language

p. 149   motion in cloth

p. 165   you could enter
       anywhere—stairs
       were all around

p. 167   corin-
         thian
         (girl)

         doric
         columns
         (man)

p. 194   holds on to
         flowering tree

p. 279   shimmering walls falling like fabric

p. 287   dome over
         a dome

p. 369   he's talking to birds

p. 398   letters
         painted
         inside

p. 405   human
         vision

p. 441   Harmony of God
         revealed in a
         moment of crisis

TRANSCRIPTION OF SELECTED MARGINALIA FOUND IN
A COPY OF *CLASSICAL LITERARY CRITICISM* PUBLISHED
BY PENGUIN IN 2000

p. xxii   explanation

p. xxxi   recognition

p. xlviii   how does it happen?

p. 20   what
about
adaptation
survival?

p. 25   why
should
we
hear

representa-
tions of
hell and death
if they are
symbolic

p. 27   denying
grief
mortals
must
be above
it

p. 50   is truth
the
essence
of
things

p. 54   fear
of
pleasure

p. 79   best is
what
you
didn't
expect

p. 86   metaphor
is
relative

p. 98   connected
to
unity

p. 106   working
your
writing

p. 122   ex's of
sublime

p. 126   ex.

p. 127   selection
        makes
        it
        sublime

p. 155   sublime is landscape

TRANSCRIPTION OF SELECTED MARGINALIA FOUND IN
A COPY OF VLADIMIR MAYAKOVSKY'S *THE BEDBUG AND
OTHER POEMS* PUBLISHED IN 1960 BY MERIDIAN BOOKS
AND PREVIOUSLY OWNED BY JOHN WISE

p. 60   Powerfull effect "cloud" thru lyrical clad in coarseness
         vulgarity, coarseness

p. 61   Identifies personal tragedy
         (jilted) w/ society's

         Down with love

         Agony of love
         attack on
         sentimental
         poets who
         cannot turn
         selves inside
         out as he is
         about to do.

p. 62   Down w/ love

         Universal depiction
         of personal
         tragedy

p. 64   adj.

p. 65   Anachronistic love

p. 67   personification

p. 71   compares self

p. 73   extended metaphor

p. 75   Down w/ art
superiority of life
to art

p. 81   wants to be
city poet —
life is better

p. 85   Down w/
social order

p. 87   2nd sec.

p. 89   cocky

p. 97   Down w/ religion

p. 105   lust religion

p. 109   ultimate rejection
hopelessness

p. 111   indictment of
woman —
suggests his own
suicide by bullet

personifi-
cation of
verse, music
to make it
live

p. 113   loneliness

p. 115   rejection
of woman
God

p. 117   God

can't do it
himself

is rejected, but will
always follow her

p. 123   Wants to escape from reality of
her rejection of him but it is
as inescapable as death. She has
killed him

Verse can give him back
life. He is giving her part of
himself, but it is too late

p. 125   to me

Indecisiveness, so seizes on absolute

p. 133   Where to
seek solitude?

Where to
seek love?

p. 135   because unsated

p. 145   scorn

p. 147   sarcasm

p. 151   anguished declaration of

p. 173   divided

religious

proud

p. 175   something familiar

p. 177   admiration

p. 181   human being almost
an anachri-
nism

attraction

p. 183   rest of world
seems stagnant in

comparison to his
striding russia

p. 187 devotion to rev.

p. 207 damaged faith showing

p. 209 supposed
to submit
accts. Of French
decadence

Answers "To His Beloved Self"

p. 211 proud 22-yr-old

p. 213 love is
passion +
physical strain
+ possessing

p. 215 love is
awareness
wrapped
in the
unaware

p. 219 Editor cannot
comprehend or
curb overwhelming
force of poet's
passions

p. 227　In review,
　　　　his poems
　　　　have served
　　　　as would a
　　　　faithful
　　　　army

p. 231　extended metaphor

p. 240　"Don't blame the mirror
　　　　if your own mug's on
　　　　crooked."

p. 271　Deviation
　　　　has
　　　　been re-
　　　　duced to
　　　　this

p. 276　Reminiscent of peddlers in 1st scene

Brethren of the Common Life) that the Christian religion is not a set of rules or ritual acts to be slavishly obeyed or performed, but a way of life in direct relationship with God. He gave to his 'fellow Germans' the Bible, hymns, catechisms, and sermons in their own language, an accomplishment which was to be the work of several men in the English reformation. His marriage and family life, taken in conjunction with his writings on the nature of the priesthood and the sacraments, helped to integrate clergy and laity. The way was thus prepared for the greater participation of the layman in the worship and government of the churches of the Protestant tradition.

Luther's positive achievements continue to the present day; so, regrettably, do some of the undesirable results of the Reformation which he began. The rift between Christians, which was a consequence of his teaching, our century can no longer accept. To have seen how it grew may help us as we in our turn contribute to history by trying to heal it.

Aug 24, 1991
12:05 a.m.

VOLUME II

TRANSCRIPTION OF THE MARGINALIA FOUND IN A USED COPY
OF PENGUIN CLASSICS' *GEOFFREY CHAUCER: LOVE VISIONS*
(*THE BOOK OF DUCHESS & THE HOUSE OF FLAME*), PUBLISHED
IN 1983 AND PREVIOUSLY OWNED BY S. MCKELVEY

p. 30   church
songs

characterizing
nother world*
as exotic

p. 64   cross

p. 81   making
himself a
"Love" poet

aspiring courtly lover
who seriously
 fails

p. 84   science of
sound

p. 85   science
of sound

p. 121   who knows
who it is
supposed to be

COMPLETE TRANSCRIPTION OF THE MARGINALIA FOUND
IN A COPY OF *NO TURNING BACK: A HOPI INDIAN WOMAN'S
STRUGGLE TO LIVE IN TWO WORLDS* BY POLIINGAYSI
QÖYAWAYMA (ELIZABETH Q. WHITE)

       end

p. 5   appreciation

p. 6   learning to
       take care
       of herself

p. 7   request

p. 13   responsibility

p. 16   contrast

p. 73   she
       could
       not
       change
       them

p. 77   he
       accepted
       her

p. 103   that's
       the
       difference

COMPLETE TRANSCRIPTION OF THE MARGINALIA FROM
THE FIRST DIALOGUE FOUND IN A COPY OF *GEORGE
BERKELEY: PRINCIPLES, DIALOGUES, AND PHILOSOPHICAL
CORRESPONDENCE*

p. 110   **28th**

p. 113   <u>intensity</u>

p. 114   heat & pain

             PAIN DISTINCT

             IMMEDIATE
             DUAL PERCEPTION

             PAIN
             NOTHING
             DISTINCT;
             INHERENT

p. 115   INTENSE
             HEAT =
             PAIN
             CANNOT E
             XIST IN
             UNP. C. S.

p. 117   DUAL
             PAIN

p. 118 TASTES

p. 119 DIFF
ERENT
TASTES

ODOURS

SOUNDS

p. 121 MOTION

p. 123 APPARENT
COLOURS

PROXIMITY
&
DISTANCE

p. 127 PRIMARY &
SECONDARY QUALITIES

?

EXTENSIOM

p. 128 DUAL
PERCEPTION

p. 129 NON-
PERCEPTION

MOTION

82

p. 130   SUCCESSION
         OF IDEAS

         SOLIDITY
         RELATIVITY

         CAUSES OF SENSATIONS NOT IMMEDIATE
         PERCEIVED ERGO NOT SENSIBLE

p. 131   ABSOLUTE &
         SENSIBLE EXTENSION

p. 132   GENERALITY
         &
         PARTICULARS

p. 133   ABSTRACTION

         NO
         ABSTRACT
         IDEAS

         ABSTRACTION
         FROM THE
         PARTICULAR

p. 134   COEXISTENCE
         OF SENSIBLE
         DUALITIES

p. 135   EXISTENCE

83

p. 136   VOLITION & PERCEPTION

p. 139   SUBSTRATUM
OF SENSIBLE
QUALITIES

p. 141   PERCEPTION
IN MIND

CONCEPTION

p. 143   CO-EXISTENCE

p. 145   <u>SUGGESTION
FROM EXPERIENCE</u>

p. 148   NOTHING BUT AN IDEA
CAN BE LIKE AN IDEA

COMPLETE TRANSCRIPTION OF THE MARGINALIA FOUND
IN A COPY OF RENÉ DESCARTES' *MEDITATIONS ON FIRST
PHILOSOPHY* PUBLISHED BY HACKETT IN 1993

p. 15   This Sucks

p. 16   evil
         deceiver

p. 20   Thinking
         thing

p. 36   Problem
         of
         Deception

p. 40   I hate this class

p. 51   substance
         dualism

00 = 935,294
01 = 928,571

105,360

_____

937,360

~~98,502~~

96, 571

p. 37   Moderation

Inwardly everything should be different but our
        outward
face should conform with the crowd

A respon-
sibility
to rescue
ppl from
cave of
shadows

Moderation

                    dainties

betoken

        penance,

p. 40   I feel the same,
         is this communism?

Plato agrees; there is
much to be learned
from ones reflection
thru someone
else

and you may be sure he is a friend of all.

Ones
own
friend
theme

COMPLETE TRANSCRIPTION OF THE MARGINALIA IN
A COPY OF *THE SUCCESS AND FAILURE OF PICASSO*
BY JOHN BERGER, PENGUIN BOOKS, 1965

p. 22 'a painting is
a sum of
destructions'

TRANSCRIPTION OF THE COMPLETE UNDERLINED PARTS IN
A USED COPY OF *THE JOURNAL OF JOHN WIENERS IS TO BE
CALLED 707 SCOTT STREET FOR BILLY HOLIDAY, 1959*,
SUN AND MOON PRESS, 1996

p. 29   **True love is an o   netic f**

SELECTED TRANSCRIPTION OF THE MARGINALIA FOUND
IN A COPY OF *ARISTOTLE'S POETICS* TRANSLATED BY
FRANCIS FURGUSSON, 1961

p. 53   again

p. 55   here's
a
goodie

p. 59   jab
slash

p. 62   plot

character

p. 63   plot

character

thought

p. 64   Character

Diction

Song

Spectacle

pooh pooh

p. 65 again

another
goodie

p. 68 Poetry— philosophical
express universal
how a person will act or speak—
to law of probability

may
happen

p. 73 rahrah

p. 79 see
p 73
"suffering"

another
rahrah

p. 81 1

crap

2

3

4

p. 91   ending
        important

p. 93   T
        h
        o
        u
        g
        h
        t

p. 113 does the end justify the
                            means

        *this is a rare one alright
        especially around here

TRANSCRIPTION OF A SELECTION FROM THE MARGINALIA
FOUND IN A COPY OF *THE SHORES OF AMERICA: THOREAU'S
INWARD EXPLORATION* BY SHERMAN PAUL, WITH THE
STAMP "THIS NO LONGER THE PROPERTY OF KING COUNTY
LIBRARY" AND PENCILED ONTO THE HALF TITLE TWO
DEFINITIONS OF TRANSCENDENTALISM AND THE WORDS,

"Lived at the pond: 1845 – 1847"

p. 23   self culture
         spiritual culture

p. 59   Sir Thomas Browne — We carry within us the
         wonder we seek without us

p. 61   FRIENDSHIP

p. 86   Electricity

p. 97   The running together of souls —

p. 104   Death

p. 116   BIRDS

p. 120   Melville

p. 121   MUSIC

p. 124   Yes

p. 199   MAINE

p. 200   MAINE

p. 202   Light/Dark Cycle

p. 213   Fish

p. 223   Awake:

p. 224   DISCOVERY

p. 227   men transiting
         all day   still

p. 266   object to
         pluck strings

p. 271   FRIENDSHIP

p. 279   crisis years— 1850–

p. 280   disconnected/random

p. 281   1850–1854 years

p. 282   Seasons:

p. 289   Autumn:

p. 290   Beginning of reflections on
                              death—

p. 291   Acceptance of each season:

p. 330   Seeds:

p. 331   Beanfield:

p. 337   Midnight fishing

p. 341   Winter:

p. 348   The Thaw

p. 353   Bhagavad-Gita

p. 357   MAINE:

TRANSCRIPTION OF THE MARGINALIA FOUND IN A COPY
OF *THE SLAB BOYS* BY JOHN BYRNE, PUBLISHED IN A
STAPLED EDITION FROM SAMUEL FRENCH, INC., 1982

p. 8   x to him

        x to slab

p. 9   x to his
        slab

        x to him

p. 10   x to him

        x to
        radio

        x to
        door

p. 11   x to him

        x to them

p. 14   x to his
        slab

        x to his
        slab

x to his
slab

p. 15 x to him

x to his

x to them

x to his
slab

p. 16 x him
to his
slab

p. 17 x to
them

x to
his
slab

x to him

p. 19 x to him

x to
slab

x to
slab

p. 20   x to
         them

p. 21   x to him

p. 22   x to
         him

p. 24   start
         to
         slab

p. 25   X

         X

p. 26   x to
         slab

         x to
         slab

         x
         between
         them

p. 27   x to him

p. 28   up
         on bench
         up

she
gets

she
does

p. 30 x to
her

p. 33 they get up

at sink

p. 35 at his
slab

p. 56 x to
him

COMPLETE TRANSCRIPTION OF THE MARGINALIA FOUND
IN A COPY OF *NOISE: THE POLITICAL ECONOMY OF MUSIC*
BY JACQUES ATTALI

p. 3   framed silence

p. 9   third reality

p. 10   circularity

p. 143 death

p. 151 thinking at music unfailing as does film
        — ie equate

COMPLETE TRANSCRIPTION OF THE MARGINALIA IN A USED COPY OF *THREE GUINEAS* BY VIRGINIA WOOLF

p. 3   women's
       equality

p. 33   small
        ant

p. 102   brol
         burning
         imagery

p. 32   from Anerca

p. 35   This cave painting doesn't
look like it represents some
magical vision of ritual
before a hunt. It looks like
a beautifully executed object
of art. An artist existed
in that cave who drew
on the walls out of
necessity—because he was
an artist...an oriental
artist at that.

p. 60   The ridiculousness of
this encounter is the
fact that I can't read
this poem—so I don't
know what it says.
Ignorance is not always
bliss. Perhaps it
just means that I
live in 1970—the
electronic man can't
fathom the medieval man
or even read into his writing

the language has evolved so
much.

p. 110   At the Great Beginning there was Non-Being…
This Non-Being was described as "e
y analogy," to a mind that is still
he whole universe surrenders
Maintain the unity of your will. Do not
sten with ears, but with the mind. o not listen with
the mind,
ut with spirit   The function of the ear ends with
hearing
hat of the mind with symbols or ideas. But the spirit
is an empty-
ness ready to receive all things."

"mirrorlike wisdom."

p. 112   its presence.

p. 113   Form is both deeply material and highly spiritual
cannot exist without a material support; it cannot be
properly expressed without invoking some
supramaterial principl

p. 114   the great way for the Great Society,
when the equilibrium of Heaven and Earth is maintained,
every-
would then be in proper position; all creatures would be

nourished   armony is creative, sameness is sterile
harmony of all the elements and ideas in a composition
    produ
eneral harmony, nd by "spiritual influence"

armony is like soup here being wate heat, sour flavoring
nd pickles, lt and peaches ith a bright fire of wood, the
armonizing all the gredients in the cooking of the fish
flesh   ter be used to help out water, who could eat it?

p. 23 For a revolutionary, failure is a springboard. As a
       source of theory it is richer than victory: it
       accumulates experience and knowledge.

p. 24 Any line that claims to be revolutionary must give
       a concrete answer to the question: How to overthrow
       the power of the capitalist state? In other words, how
       to break its backbone, the army,

p. 27 The end of an epoch, the epoch of relative class
       equilibrium. The beginning of another, that of total
       class warfare, excluding compromise solutions and
       shared power.

p. 30 Self-defense does not exclude insurrection, but
       such an insurrection will always be local and will not
       seek to extend its action to the entire country. Self
       defense is partial; revolutionary guerrilla warfare
       aims at total war by combining under its hegemony
       all forms of struggle at all points with the territory.

p. 31 Self-defense is nothing more than a small part of
       a whole, with special characteristics. It is never
       possible to conceive of a self-defense as complete
       in itself, i.e. as a region where the popular forces
       attempt to defend themselves against enemy attack,
       while the entire zone beyond remains free of

disturbances. In such a case, the *foco* would be localized, cornered, and defeated, unless there occurred an immediate passage to the first phase of the people's war, in other words, to guerrilla warfare.

p. 45 Thus, self-defense reduces the guerrilla force to an inclusively tactical role and deprives it of the possibility of making even the slightest strategic revolutionary contribution. By choosing to operate at this level, it may be able to provide protection for the population for a limited time. But in the long run, the opposite is true: self-defense undermines the security of the civilian population.

Allowing oneself to be attacked or limiting oneself to passive defense is to place oneself in the position of being unable to protect the population and to expose one's own forces to attrition. On the other hand, to seek for ways to attack the enemy is to put him on the permanent defensive, to exhaust him and prevent him from expanding his activities, to wrest the initiative from him, and to impede his search operations. Here we have the best way to fulfill our glorious mission of protecting the population.

TRANSCRIPTION OF MARGINALIA FOUND IN LECTURE FIVE
("THE HERO AS MAN OF LETTERS") IN A USED COPY OF
ON HEROS, HERO-WORSHIP, AND THE HEROIC IN HISTORY BY
THOMAS CARLYLE, UNIVERSITY OF NEBRASKA PRESS, 1966

p. 154   Past
         &
         Present

p. 156   the
         thing

p. 160   Book
         &
         Myth

p. 162   University
         as
         Books

p. 165   Thought
         is as
         a Book

p. 171   World
         Machine

TRANSCRIPTION OF SELECTED MARGINALIA FOUND IN
A COPY OF *THE CLOUDS* BY ARISTOPHANES, PUBLISHED IN
1994 BY CROFT CLASSICS, AND PREVIOUSLY OWNED BY
MARK FENDER

p. 5   Weak
        comedy!

p. 8   view of
        farmers

        view of
        philos.

p. 9   *NOPE!

p. 14   religion

p. 15   ets. =

p. 19   Rejecting
        gods

        Not passionate
        protest

p. 21   *Good line!

p. 22   mocking
        play
        structure

p. 26 attack on lack of piety conventional

p. 27 this play seems very
       conservative

       mocking
       education

p. 29 Funny
       in English

p. 31 No
       ques

p. 33 Refuting
       Gods

       *

p. 35 not so! Soph.

p. 37 old vs.
       new

p. 40 incredible
       translation
       work!

p. 42 Bawdy

       Pederasty
       –yuck

p. 44   Ad for
artist! Play

p. 50   For the common man—middle class
conservatives

soc.
ques

p. 51   choral
warning

p. 52   old
vs.
new

p. 53   hypocrisy

p. 54   stupidity

soc
ques

p. 57   Mock soc.

COMPLETE TRANSCRIPTION OF THE MARGINALIA
IN COPY OF *SIX NON LECTURES* BY EE CUMMINGS,
HARVARD UNIVERSITY PRESS, 1953

p. 49   WOW!

COMPLETE TRANSCRIPTION OF THE PENCILED MARGINALIA
IN AN EXCEPTIONALLY INKED-UP COPY OF CHRISTOPHER
MARLOWE'S *DR. FAUSTUS*, PUBLISHED IN A DOVER THRIFT
EDTION, 1994

p. 3   acad
    disciplines

    philosophy
    too easy
    for him

    medicine—but
    must study
    physic (physician)

p. 4   he is great
    already
    lazy. but
    if only he
    could

    lawyer—

    libral=
    free

    black
    magic

p. 8   food

p. 11   heavens

        wandering

p. 13   unfortunate

p. 15   Dom

p. 16   By the mass

p. 17   that's that

p. 19   fatal
        loss
        of
        life
        (SIN)

        What good is it

        Worthy of hatred

        domain

p. 20   how you that
        torture others
        have only pain?

        my own

        lucifer

        "

p. 23   too smart for
        his own good

p. 25   still has second thoughts

p. 32   food

        food

        sum of
        all good
        things
        (ideal of
        everything
        good)

p. 35   incomparable

p. 37   person who
        draws you a
        drink (bartender)

p. 44   bole

p. 47   became

        food

p. 49   seems to
        me

p. 50   horrible

        evil

p. 51   attitude (sad)

p. 52   unfortunate
         luckless

         (zues)

         as a lightning
         bolt

p. 53   if I had

         then I would
         have lived forever

         eating too much

p. 55   ~~tagging~~
         locking

p. 56   having luck

         Aristotle
         recognition

         alive

         good at academics

         formerly

COMPLETE TRANSCRIPTION OF THE MARGINALIA FOUND IN
THE FIRST TEN PAGES OF A COPY OF *UNDER MILK WOOD* BY
DYLAN THOMAS, PUBLISHED BY NEW DIRECTIONS

p. 1   fade out
        on song

        Scene 1

        GIANNI

        sea
        NOISES

        reverberation
        of the
        'sh'

        c.l.
        leaves

        1st group
        starts
        glacial

        2nd
        GROUP

p. 2   2ND
        GROUP

3RD
GROUP
MOVES

IN FORMATION INHALE/EXHALE

DONNA

START
CREAKY

SEA
SOUNDS
FADED

OUT

GLACIAL
MOVEMENT

MORE BEHIND

TERESA

p. 3 IN FULL line

ear locking R to shoulder

start to move to sleep

done
w/
formation

trail
off after
light

Go towards
DONNA Maggie E

waves

Davey Jones
lock

Scene 2

truly has deep love

for A—
town.

*How tortured
he is.

*Set the town
up for this
memory.

p. 4 light
comes
up.

p. 7 Scene 3

make
about Audience

innuendo

<u>ME</u>

<u>based</u>

look @ pacing for
rythem
b, t, k, p,

<u>plosive</u>

create
alive

p. 9 Scene 4

<u>ADAM</u>

ADAM: I fade into the background.

p. 7 blood-

red

crucifix

carved gilt unmade

mitre and gilded cope

tragedian's cothurni

Our heart is our undoing

p. 10 I saw the greedy lodging for

transgression

You live in evil

p. 15 I want to see

hot tears gush from your lovely eyes.

p. 17 That's why I'm dead. I inhabit that region of exact

freedom Hell

p. 20 One cannot commit evil in evil

judge

p. 21   I wouldn't take the liberty of asking you your opinions.
        Everyone is free, and I'm not concerned with politics.

p. 23   My handsome mare

p. 24   It's quite
        job dressing a victorious general who's to be buried

p. 28   Leather

p. 30   A smile means doubt

p. 31   the orgy

                    seed never ripens in you

                        the orgies of your heart

p. 34   The Grand Balcony
        the most artfu   et the most decent house of
        illusions

p. 43   What's one illusion more or
                less!

p. 49   you want to merge your life with one long
                unreal

                            Is life anything els?

p. 50   But supposing they let themselves be carried beyond th
        gam   mean if they get so involved in it that th
        destroy and replace everything

You mean into reality?

p. 55 Black

Black

p. 61 It's make-believe

a fake corpse

haunted by a quest of immobility

p. 64 o gaze at the world tranquilly and acce
sponsibility for your gaze

p. 65 What significance has that rag whe
ou're about to penetrate into the providential fixity

p. 67 Do
ou tremble if there's no authority above you to decide

p. 69 mirrors will reflect to

the image of a dead man

p. 73 A return to order   return to classicism

p. 75 It's a true image   born of a false spectacle

The massacre   re revels wherein the
people indulge to their heart's content in the pleasure of
hating us.

p. 76   Every
niche has its statue

p. 77   you think
we're going to be satisfied with make-believe to the end o
our days

p. 79   are you going to use what we
              epresent or are we
              going to use you to serve what we represent

                            ours was a happy
tate

p. 83   above God are you without whom God
            would be nothing

              to seek qui   decisive ways a manifes
           saintliness

p. 84 Love of God was hidden there
                           a concern for justice

               bravery and military glory and the heroi
deed that haunted you

p. 85 The Queen attains her reality when she withdraws, absent
herself r die

              Their only hope lies in the utter collapse

p. 88   the mountain is sacre

p. 89   Life's starting up agai
little by little   as before

p. 90   you ask
questions that aren't in the scenario

p. 92   And go wher   Into life

p. 94   Though my image be castrated in
every brothel in the worl   I remain intac

p. 96   You must now go home   where everythin you can be
quite sure   will be falser than here

extinguishes the last light

p. 126   <u>Life is</u>   <u>forever</u>

p. 127

<u>Consciousness of shipwreck
stitutes salvation</u>

creation

<u>mere administering of wealth he had
received</u>

p. 157   words-in-freedom, in this con

                        force and profundity, naturally

          ustrations, by   ns free, expressive orthograp

          y, the synoptic tables of lyric values and design

                        ords in freedom manage to make u

                        rt of communicative exuberance and

          that is one of the characteristics of the southern rac

                        ccents, voice, and mimcry that has shown up

                        ors and brilliant talkers find its natural exp

          rtions of typographic characters that repr

                        don become the lyric and transfigured pr

          mal magnetism.

TRANSCRIPTION OF THE UNDERLINED PARTS OF A PAGE
IN A COPY OF *VISION AND DESIGN* BY ROGER FRY FOUND
IN A COPY SOLD BY BRENTANO'S, NEW YORK

p. 48   practical visi

curiosity vision

TRANSCRIPTION OF SELECTED MARGINALIA FOUND
IN A COPY OF PLATO'S *THEAETETUS*, FROM A STUDENT
GREAT BOOKS EDITION, THE GREAT BOOKS FOUNDATION,
CHICAGO, 1956

p. 30   Good
question

p. 31   see
oppos-
ite
page

p. 32   <u>THE</u>
question

p. 33   tricky

p. 34   quite
a
teacher!
<u>winning</u>

p. 35   How
Human

p. 44   DELIGHTFUL

p. 45   TRUE

p. 46 DESCRIPTION
OF
LAWYER

p. 47 DESCRIPTION
OF
POLITICAL
CLUBS

p. 48 PHILOSOPHERS
DESCRIBED

p. 49 PHILOSOPHERS
DESCRIBED

p. 59 WHY
SO

?

p. 60 I
DON'T GET
IT

p. 61 There
is no
answer
here
for
me
I
Don't
get it

p. 65   2 words
        used
        for
        same
        meaning

        good

p. 66   meaning
        ?

        oh!?

p. 67   And nobody has done so
        to this day ! ! ! !

p. 70   pretty
        cute

COMPLETE TRANSCRIPTION OF THE MARGINALIA FOUND
IN A COPY OF ANTON CHEKHOV'S *THREE SISTERS*,
TRANSLATED BY MICHAEL FRAYN AND PUBLISHED IN
1989 BY METHUEN, LONDON

1C   compare & contrast their
tusenbach   views
vershin   of the
          future

p. 5   good talk from aristocracy
gets
a
job
and
hates
it

p. 6   russian (Bolshevik) revolution

COMPLETE TRANSCRIPTION OF THE UNDERLINING IN A
COPY OF *THE POSTMODERNS*, THE NEW AMERICAN POETRY
REVISED, PAGE ONE HUNDRED AND NINETY-EIGHT
("WHY I AM NOT A PAINTER," BY FRANK O'HARA)

p. 198   orange
orange

orange
orange

and life

orang

ORANGES

COMPLETE TRANSCRIPTION OF MARGINALIA IN A
1974 VINTAGE EDITION OF *MARXISM AND ART: ESSAYS CLASSIC
AND CONTEMPORARY*, BY MARTY SOLOMON, AND FOUND IN
A PENNSYLVANIA BOOKSTORE

p. 84   **Vision**

COMPLETE TRANSCRIPTION OF MARGINALIA IN A
1968 CLARENDON BIOGRAPHIES EDITION OF *ERASMUS &*
LUTHER BY ROSEMARY DEVONSHIRE JONES ON THE LAST
PAGE OF TEXT

p. 90   **Aug 24, 1991**
         12:05 a.m.

COMPLETE TRANSCRIPTION OF THE MARGNINALIA IN
A USED COPY OF *VLADIMIR TATLIN AND THE RUSSIAN
AVANTE-GARDE* BY JOHN MILNER, FOUND IN THE
CLEARANCE BIN AT HALF PRICE BOOKS

p. 211   warhol

COMPLETE TRANSCRIPTION OF THE MARGINALIA FOUND IN
A USED COPY OF MARY ANNE STANIZOWSKI'S *BELIEVING IS
SEEING*, PUBLISHED BY PENGUIN IN 1995

p. 120   **pop?**

                kitch?

COMPLETE TRANSCRIPTION OF THE MARGINALIA FOUND
IN A USED COPY OF *DUTCHMAN AND THE SLAVE*, TWO PLAYS
BY LEROI JONES, PUBLISHED IN 1964

p.3 writing
     on
     wall

p.14 <u>Scavenger</u>

p.29 con.
      camps.

p.30 Reference To
      Adam & Eve

p.73 whiteman

THE COMPLETE CIRCLED SECTIONS (AND BRIEF FITS
OF MARGINALIA) IN A USED COPY OF *UNDISCOVERED
COUNTRY, DAS WEITE LAND* BY ARTHUR SCHNITZLER,
IN AN ENGLISH VERSION BY TOM STOPPARD, PUBLISHED
BY FABER AND FABER IN 1980

p. 15   Friedrich takes from each according to
        his needs, you see...

p. 16   Awful moment for the manservant. What h
        with the cigars? Did he leave then?

        A: Mama believes in historical precision

p. 24   suppose you think I do
        him? But in my opinion, yearning is a necessary part
        he soul's economy. Relationships are all the better for i
        In an ideal world more and more people would see less
        less of each other. Anyway we can go back with Joey to
        England, and you can decide then if you want to come
        me or stay with the boy through the winter.
        I'd rather you took it as final
        ICH: Final? Look, what's the matter with you, G
        're behaving very oddly.

p. 32   there to laugh at? He at least takes it
        ously. In my opinion a good tennis player is a no
        pecimen of humanity than a mediocre poet or g
        (To OTTO.) Well, aren't I right?
        : (TO GENIA) Well now, when is
        enia

p. 36   I can't say you are wrong with that. But I ca
imagine what you're suggesting. Erna! A girl I have
on my knee.
E: What difference does that make? There are girls
of whom that can be said

st beginning.
is more to life—women to m
Oh, yes—there are spaces between them.
interesting. If one has the time and if one is in the
one builds factories, conquers nations, writes sympho
becomes a millionaire…but, believe me, all that is
to fill in the time. Life is for you! Life is for you
: (Shaking her h

p. 38   R: Alas your kind concern comes too late. Of cour
can't deny that, like all men, as you say…but not an
longer…in my case. A squalid affair has no appeal to
I would disgust myself.
What a gentleman you

p. 39   ICH: To speak of being familiar with a loved one is a
contradiction in terms…Lovers should be referred to a
constant unfamiliars…
Or members of the fair sex if you

p. 44   , you see, the thought that your virtue…
thing so abstract—at least compared to the terribl
eversible fact of death—that your virtuousness drov
marvelous man to his grave, that to me is ghastly. Y
I can't put it any other way…it'll pass, of course,
feeling…in time…in the mountains…and if

apart for a few weeks...but at the moment, it
and I can't do anything about it...Yes, Ge
have me—Other men would feel differentl

p.61   AIGNER: Why I betrayed her? *You ask me?* Hav
ever thought what a strange uncharted country is
behavior? So many contradictions find room i
and deceit...loyalty and betrayal...wors
yet longing for another, or severa

p.65   nd that's an end of it, They can still get Mauer back. I
have no interest in making a public spectacle of myself
(A Gong sounds. The HIKER who has gone to slee

p.76   e's also a friend.
Do you think he still is?
EDRICH: Yes. Friendship is above incident. These things d
depend on...events. He could shoot me dead and it
still be his friend he's shot.
ERNA: What is the business that's so important?
RIEDRICH: Come on my sweetheart! A wife c
quisitive. Anywa

p.79   e more secure.
m beginning to find you amusing.
DRICH: Well, that's something. Since certainty is unattain-
able, entertainment value is the only justification for
conversation
UER: I'd be able to get the truth from Erna herself.

p.83   o allow you or forbid you sti
rau! (MAUER *turns back to* GENIA) and they em

bye, dear Doctor!—And…please let me
piece of advice to go with you—Don't take it too
would be silly for you, who se life at its most truly
erious, to take seriously these foolish games. Well, that's
all that love affairs are, Doctor, believe me. And once you'
accepted that, they're very enjoyable to watch even to tak
part in.

MAUER: Once you have accepted that   STAR WARS

GENIA: Lies? Can one have lies in a game? That's calle
all part of the fun

ER: A game? Oh yes, if that's how it wa
nia, I would have nothi

p. 86 hat's right—I couldn't give a damn ab
at. But I won't be made to look a fool.
(FRIEDRICH *turns from* GENIA *and foll*
TANZADES

epitaph

p. 93 : *(Still motionless)*
A: *(Now, a little nearer to him)* Believe me, Friedrich, I l
you, I belong to you.
FRIEDRICH: I belong to no one on this earth. No one. Nor
wish to…
Y'S VOICE: *(In the garden)* Mother! Father!

pg 15, 16, 32, 36, 39, 44
61, 79, 83, 86, 93

38 ma
76 friendship

comes undone. His groin is e
tender spot. A forbidden corn
manager. I saw just such a velv
once. Amorous currents mus
secretaries and office girls at

He washes himself like a
around, snorts, makes noises.
the hollow of his hands. Mos
before it reaches his armpits.
are full and clean. The lather,
like a pancake. Sometimes the
tears at his eyelids with his th
gargling with such zest that, un
and raise their heads.

The morning is quiet and
There are flower boxes on all
milion of this year's blooms is

(Things don't like me. Fur
Once the sharp corner of som
me. My relations with my blar
Soup, given to me, never cools
or a collar button—falls off the
some almost unmovable piec

Material World (?)

VOLUME III

TRANSCRIPTION OF MARGINALIA FOUND IN A COPY
OF *ENVY AND OTHER WORKS* BY YURI OLESHA, PUBLISHED
BY NORTON IN 1991 AND PREVIOUSLY OWNED BY
KATE PORTERFIELD

p. 2 Material
      World (?)

p. 34 looking through
       him

p. 56 Ivan

p. 58 Tree

p. 69 – pigs
       – blue
       – green
       – trees

p. 72 "New
        Man"

p. 80 Don
       Quixote

p. 97 Ivan
       vs
       The
       Struct-
       ure

[inside front cover]

1B	Drapo	✔	1.	Ruzzuto	SS	R
2B	Doerr	✔	2.	Kell	3B	R
3B	Kell	✔	3.	WIlliams	LF	L
SS	Ruzzuto	✔	4.	Drapo	1B	R
LF	Williams	✔	5.	Doby	CF	R
RF	Evers		6.	Evers	RF	L
C	Berra		7.	Berra	C	L
			8.	Doerr	2B	R

[inside back cover]

LF	Harkins	5´10˝	✔
RF	Armom	5´7˝	✔
C	McDowell	6´4˝	✔
LF	Walsh	6´2˝	✔
RF	Daley	6´2˝	?
	Braca	6´	✔
	Gallegher	6´2˝	✔
	Rose	5´11˝	✔
	Robben	5´9˝	✔
	Curtim	6´3˝	?

COMPLETE TRANSCRIPTION OF THE BRACKETED PARTS
IN A COPY OF GERTRUDE STEIN'S *LECTURES IN AMERICA*,
PUBLISHED BY RANDOM HOUSE, 1935

p. 95   [Nervousness is the certain proof that the emotion
         of the one seeing and the emotion of the thing seen
         do not progress together]

COMPLETE TRANSCRIPTION OF MARGINALIA FOUND IN A
COPY OF *AN ANTHOLOGY OF CONCRETE POETRY*, EDITED BY
EMMETT WILLIAMS AND PUBLISHED BY SOMETHING ELSE
PRESS, INC. 1967

p. 332   *

p. 333   *

p. 336   *

p. 340   *

                *

                *

                *

p. 341   *

TRANSCRIPTION OF THE MARGINALIA FOUND IN A
LIBRARY COPY OF BERNADETTE MAYER'S *MIDWINTER DAY*,
NEW DIRECTIONS, 1982

p. 1   you were
         staying in
         the mirror
         with me

p. 2   I'm made
         of you

         I was alone in the dreams
         dressing room.

p. 6   though would she agree
         with that?
         continuation/
         start of a new
         idea
         fleeting
         how she
         dreams
         /near

p. 7   everything
         seemed good

         not so fleeting

         dream = meditation

"Not only sleep but on
awakening"
weathering
in dream or
reality?
confused? or
feeling over loaded?

p. 8 * * *

p. 9 "bereft dream
cakes"

p. 10 trying to
make
sense of
it

p. 11 *dream which
reminds her
of another
dream
Δ
also a
dream
(within itself)
Δ
dream within
a dream?
Δ
or an
entanglement

of dreams
Δ

a <u>knot</u>?
Δ
which she is
trying to
untangle

p. 13   "seemed to make sense"

"Next
dream

trying to define those
dreams

TRANSCRIPTION OF THE COMPLETE MARGINALIA FOUND
IN A USED COPY OF RANDA DUBNICK'S *THE STRUCTURE
OF OBSCURITY: GERTRUDE STEIN, LANGUAGE, AND CUBISM*,
PUBLISHED BY THE UNIVERSITY OF ILLINOIS PRESS IN 1984

p. 4   O.K.

Bad

Good

So-So

Maybe

p. 5   Never

Fuck it

[inside cover]

> if you don't start piles, they can't
> grow!
>
> p 71–72 Yard sales

p. 1   *
> – debt
> – responsibility
> more to
> clean/do

p. 16   step #1
> step #2

p. 17   step
> #2
> (cont)
> step
> #3

p. 18   step
> #
> 4

p. 23   counter

p. 24 **p. 17**

p. 29 **2/3**
1/3
1/2
1/2
& internet

p. 30 storage
classroom

p. 33 why is it
still this
way?
china

v35 (what you dream for your
home to be.)

p. 38 china

p. 39 <u>a roof</u>

p. 40 cards

p. 51 No
no
tired &
overwhelmed
relaxed&
comfortable
"Like it's a disaster"
"Like it's restful"
overwhelmed

"like it's opened"
p 80–81

p. 54   the Reality
        Me   He
          Them
          visions

p. 63   No = trash
        No = trash
        No = trash
        Yes = keep &
        Donations/

p. 64   Larry's
        van
        seat

p. 67   A weekend plan!
        B
        A
        B

p. 68   Attic

p. 70   3
        4
        5
        Attic
        *
        6

p. 97 Remove!
      – games
      – laundry
      – old
      clothes
      – trash
      – toys

p. 108 Laundry
       baskets on
       attic steps

TRANSCRIPTION OF MARGINALIA FOUND IN THE GEORGE
HERBERT SECTION OF A COPY OF *THE OXFORD BOOK OF
SEVENTEENTH CENTURY VERSE*, PRINTED IN 1946 AT
THE CLARENDON PRESS AND PREVIOUSLY OWNED
BY JOYCE GOLD

p. 361   subj. the day of gladness
may pass as a hymn
as in affliction
beauty
warmlight

p. 362   try to compete
with this day

Same as L. 10

p. 363   Dull + dry as
time eclipsed
undecided
stars name for
ideal + glorious
end
excitability

suffering tone

p. 365   Resolve of reason
checked by love –
I can't take another
master, fixed I

am in love to
thee, I know no greater
punishment than to
be forbidden to love.

Theme: Broods for repose that is always the
same

p. 367 Theme: Human love makes its poetry labored +
artificial, divine love shall make mine swift
+ simple

are becoming

– chair

p. 368 – is washed
Coloring
Metaphor — man to window
                    God to sun

p. 369 sunimage

p. 370 Thru his lif

(2 meanings)

spin.-knows
where to get spin.
guidance

p. 371 tone-light
       Springy
       Exultant
       Resolvefull tone
       dispositions
       fainting
       sluggish

       Theme: Life as action

p. 372 Theme: The construction of man as
       clumsily managed by himself

       Light pillars
       that can't stand

       with leaves
       they tried to
       protect themselves

p. 373 bad
       burning building down
       sweet repeated
       color too bright makes
       yields, bends, glues way
       live coals final
       conflagration

p. 374 wither of flowers
       like death
       heavenly joys
       poison

corrected

p. 376   conceit wood
          Heart / frame

p. 378   intentionally shut eyes
          ring with
          fig of skull
          manufactured
          fears no longer
          stop breaking away

p. 379   Theme: God has made, us for himself
          man's heart is restless until it finds rest in God
          dissatisfaction with
          goods-conscience
          Theme-God
          has made us for
          himself and our
          hearts are restless
          until it finds
          rest in thee

p. 380   flower-subj
          to God's word +
          law
          uplifting itself
          toward
          spiritual anger

p. 381   must be sound
          from him

music
noise contrasted with
music

p. 382
fragrance
Theme: Love should have reciprocal ^ to lover + to
loved

p. 383 when crushed, yields odor-

p. 385 theme: pain of absence
– readjustment of a poem
sel. poem from
love"

p. 386 apostrophe
– hollow sound
– Groans of last
sickness

p. 387 body in grove
cocoon
thru grief + dust

p. 388 tone-humble
faith
(hell)
muster
communion

COMPLETE TRANSCRIPTION OF MARGINALIA FOUND ON
THE TITLE PAGE OF A COPY OF HENRY FIELDING'S
THE JOURNAL OF A VOYAGE TO LISBON, PUBLISHED BY
PENGUIN BOOKS IN 1996

10
16 –
20 – fruits – food ?
22 – death sentence
77 – appetite
79 – wind –
93 – ship/body.
107 – end – good supper.

p. 3   ABOUT THE END?

p. 4   future : doom

p. 39   1.
        How earth was formed
        2.
        3.

p. 40   4.
        5.
        6.

p. 41   7.
        8.
        9.
        10.

p. 43   11.
        12.

p. 110 unable to tolerate
        sun

p. 132 find conversation inside grave – around

p. 134   rebirth

p. 141   transformation

p. 146   ring

p. 148   F. as serpent

p. 149   raven

p. 152   S. conceals name

p. 153   (note)

p. 169   S. slain

p. 170   B's laugh

p. 182   B's laugh

         B's story

p. 184   B's suicide

p. 201   old tales

p. 211   plays harp in snake pit

SELECTED UNDERLINED PARTS FOUND IN A USED COPY OF
WAR WITH THE NEWTS BY KAREL ČAPEK, PUBLISHED BY
BANTAM BOOKS, 1964

p. 7   and all clearly expecting to be filmed

p. 10   after all, when you're naked you've nowhere to put your
        Hands except on your own shoulders

p. 11   As if there was some
        kind of a dam below the water

p. 31   Some of them tried their own to take a shell
        to pieces with a bit of old shell that was lying about. Well,
        that struck me as very queer, my lad. No animal can use
        tools; it's no use, after all. An animal is only part of nature.

p. 34   I had to call them by different
        names, you know, so that I could write about them in my
        book.

p. 36   I gave them my word that if they would
        bring me the pearl shells I would give them harpoons and
        knives in exchange, so that they could defend themselves,
        see

p. 53   What of that: there are some obvious and
        nonsensical things that men will do as long as the world
        turns roun

p. 129 I lost that game. It suddenly struck me that every move

in chess was old and had already been played by someone.
Perhaps our history has already been played too, and we
shift our figures with the same moves to the same checks
as in times long past

p. 134   Besides, people never regard what
          serves them and is good for them as in any way
          mysterious, but only what does them harm or threatens
          them

p. 136   In this respect it might make an excel-
          lent, almost indomitable animal for the purposes of war
          unfortunately, against this stands his peacefulness and
                  natural
          defenselessness

p. 201   But let us not be afraid of this; to-day
          no creature that is going to succeed to the history of man-
          kind will repeat its suicidal madness.

p. 238   Must Nature always be
          asked to straighten out the mess that man has made

COMPLETE TRANSCRIPTION OF THE UNDERLINED PARTS
IN A COPY OF MICHAEL HEIZER'S *SCULPTURE IN REVERSE*,
PUBLISHED BY THE MUSEUM OF CONTEMPORARY ART
IN 1984

p. 38   Large sculpture ultimately creates its own environment because of its size. It's different than taking
a number of big paintings and hanging them around
the walls of a room to create an environment because
the room is still an environment, the paintings are on
the walls

When I went to the
bottom of the *Munich Depression* I looked up and
realized the view of the landscape was gone; I realized I had just erased landscape

COMPLETE TRANSCRIPTION OF THE MARGINALIA FOUND IN
A COPY OF WILLIAM C. SEITZ'S *HANS HOFFMAN*, PUBLISHED
BY THE MUSEUM OF MODERN ART IN 1963

p. 14   They
used
no
depth

p. 21   depth

p. 53   Tension

COMPLETE READABLE MARGINALIA FOUND IN A LIBRARY
COPY OF ELIZABETH SMART'S *BY GRAND CENTRAL STATION I
SAT DOWN AND WEPT*, EDITIONS POETRY LONDON, 1945

[inside cover]

       from one end
       to another, the
       lie of her sex...

p. 7   terrible
       construction

p. 9   Exactly what
       is wrong
       with this
       child of
       bedlam!

p. 13 Doesn't
       make sense!
       Terrible!

       Impotence,
       too!

       this begins
       to read like
       a case-history—
       psychopathology
       literally flows

through its
pages –

it is short
of impossible
to believe
that these
feelings
could
emerge from
the same
person
who wrote
the algolagnic
reminiscences
of the preceeding
pages. But,
as with Voltairine
de Cleyre, the
real person
has at the
very depths,
covered +
corrupted by so much
dirt + slime. But in
E.S.'s case, it seems
that her exclamations, above, are
no more than superficial, prompted
by intense guilt feelings

p. 18   curious
very
curious

p. 30   compare
        this Alison's
        poem on
        pity

p. 31   pure
        sadism –

        vulgarity –

        that's
        what
        all the
        cheap
        movie-
        heroines
        exclaim
        too!

p. 32   Always
        blood, but
        not the blood
        of the heart,
        living blood
        that is, but
        that which
        is spelled:
        dead blood.

p. 35   contempt-
        ible
        bitch!

p. 36   How
         you go
         whoring,
         period!

         fantasy,
         after
         fantasy!

p. 37   the five senses do not need negligees no
         the reason to dream up freak ways of doing "it"
         this is more of your vulgarity and algolagnia
         leading you astray, Miss Smart—

p. 38   suicidal
         drives (?)

p. 54   Lies,
         lies!
         lies!

[end page]

a thoroughly <u>wicked</u> book!

COMPLETE TRANSCRIPTION OF THE MARGINALIA IN
A 1985 PENGUIN EDITION OF *LES LIASONS DANGEREUSES*
BY CHODERLOS DE LACLOS

p. 33   Merlevil
         had
         said
         opp-
         osite

p. 20   propri-
         ety

p. 254   human
         behavior
         that's
         what
         they
         do

p. 32   d she had
          emotional blindspots
          that were glari

p. 33   this experience
          outside of
          language somewhere

COMPLETE TRANSCRIPTION OF THE MARGINALIA FOUND
IN A LIBRARY COPY OF LYN HEJINIAN'S *MY LIFE*,
PUBLISHED BY SUN AND MOON IN 1987

p. 7   Stein
        allusion

p. 13   clearly
        stated

p. 14   how are
        these functioning?

p. 16   everyone does
        this

p. 18   ?

COMPLETE TRANSCRIPTION OF MARGINALIA FOUND
ON THE TITLE PAGE OF A USED COPY OF *OFF THE WALL:*
INTERVIEWS WITH PHILIP WHALEN, FOUR SEASONS
FOUNDATION, BOLINAS, 1978

7/28/78

Tobias
(End-noted)
joint rev. with
Decrompessions,
if worthy

COMPLETE TRANSCRIPTION OF THE MARGINALIA FOUND
IN A USED COPY OF *THE ESSENTIAL SHAKESPEARE*,
PUBLISHED BY CAMBRIDGE IN 1962 AND PREVIOUSLY
OWNED BY JOHN DOVER WILSO

p. 9   way to the place of crucifixion

COMPLETE TRANSCRIPTION OF BLACK PEN MARGINALIA
FOUND IN A USED COPY OF *THE FIGURE IN THE CARPET AND
OTHER STORIES* BY HENRY JAMES, PUBLISHED IN 1995
BY PENGUIN CLASSICS AND PREVIOUSLY OWNED BY
ROBERT WICKS

p. 395   tradition=the lot

p. 363   that was not what I meant at all
          that was not it at all

COMPLETE TRANSCRIPTION OF MARGINALIA FOUND
IN A USED COPY OF A COLLECTION OF ESSAYS BY
GEORGE ORWELL, HBJ, 1953 PREVIOUSLY OWNED BY
MELANIE MORIS

p. 144   just for
         power

p. 156   elephant shot so he wouldn't
         feel like a fool

TRANSCRIPTION OF SELECTED MARGINALIA FOUND IN
A USED COPY OF DOSTOEVSKY'S *THE DOUBLE*, TRANSLATED
BY EVELYN HARDEN AND PUBLISHED BY ARDIS IN 1985

p. 45   mechanically
         reinserted into
         narrative

p. 46   out of
         control

p. 52   of
         thunder

p. 59   u
         n
         c
         a
         n
         n
         y

p. 142   undecidability
         of text

p. 145   betrayal

p. 147   ✔
         ✔
         ✔

p. 158   **dream premonition**

p. 174   **split shoes**

TRANSCRIPTION OF SELECTED MARGINALIA FOUND IN
A LIBRARY COPY OF *WHEN I SAY NO, I FEEL GUILTY* BY
MANUEL J. SMITH, AND PUBLISHED BY DIAL PRESS IN 1975

p. 10   "child"

          ur or

p. 17   parents join
          child.

p. 57   – Gordon op-
          posed

p. 207   but I do get home late and thats what you have to
          deal with.

          – then she'll run away +
          that's not negotiable

p. 261   exist

p. 40   what's so
         different
         about it?

p. 41   good

p. 42   ?

p. 50   absent
         ha

p. 59   reading over
         & over
         again

p. 77   *gods

         *boys

p. 165   what?

TRANSCRIPTION OF SELECTED MARGINALIA FOUND IN
A LIBRARY COPY OF WILLIAM BARRETT'S *IRRATIONAL MAN*
AND PUBLISHED BY HEINMANN IN 1958

p. 3   or he
        finds
        himself
        a bug!
          ∆
        kafka

p. 162 M<u>asks</u>

p. 186 tree?
        (ick)

p. 203 TIME IS
        RELATIVE-
        WE MEASURE
        IT BY THE
        CHANGE OF
        THINGS—
        DIFFERENT
        CHANGES
        DIFF. TIME
        (FRAMES OF
        REFERENCE).

p. 207   r
                e
                a
                d
                !

p. 211 SURE
        IT IS
        THERE—
        WE MUST
        OPEN EYES
        TO IT
        PASSIVELY.

p. 227 But
        there
        has to
        be a stage
        w/ possibil-
        ities

p. 244 see
        Sarte

COMPLETE TRANSCRIPTION OF MARGINALIA FOUND IN
A LIBRARY COPY OF *SHAME: THE EXPOSED SELF* BY MICHAEL
LEWIS AND PUBLISHED BY THE FREE PRESS IN 1992

p. 128   forgetting is
denial

Felecia's method:
Drop the class

p. 132   How can the teacher
encourage confession

shifting position of another Katerina   what it takes to be
in computer course

p. 133   imagined
communities

p. 134   but this is guilt

p. 136   this is
guilt

?

p. 174   value of shame

COMPLETE TRANSCRIPTION OF ENGLISH MARGINALIA
FOUND IN A COPY OF *LOVE AND WILL* BY ROLLO MAY,
PUBLISHED BY W. W. NORTON & CO., 1969

p. 11   same values . inner values .

p. 40   1969

p. 52   <u>news</u> odd — what if
         the 1950's

TRANSCRIPTION OF SELECTED MARGINALIA FOUND IN
A USED COPY OF *MARCEL PROUST: A LIFE* BY EDWARD
WHITE, PUBLISHED BY PENGUIN IN 1999

p. 6   voilá

p. 7   YOUPIN

p. 9   5´6˝

p. 15   OMG

p. 36   sexual urges

p. 37   sexual strings

p. 41   Mon Dieu

p. 49   Pastiche

COMPLETE TRANSCRIPTION OF MARGINALIA FOUND IN A
USED COPY OF D.H. LAWRENCE'S *PSYCHOANALYSIS AND THE
UNCONSCIOUS AND FANTASIA OF THE UNCONSCIOUS* PUBLISHED
BY PENGUIN IN 1960

p. 49   ?

p. 88   yikes!

p. 100   why not?

p. 102   My God!

p. 109   Okay!

p. 167   It's always
         allowed

TRANSCRIPTION OF SELECTED MARGINALIA FOUND IN A
USED COPY OF *FIVE PEARS OR PEACHES* BY REGINALD GIBBONS,
PUBLISHED BY BROKEN MOON PRESS, 1991

p. 3   long sentences

p. 7   long sentences   ordinary everyday
        tangents
        metaphor — sandpaper, peas / peaches

p. 28   his
        opinion

TRANSCRIPTION OF MARGINALIA FOUND IN A LIBRARY
COPY OF *INDIVIDUAL BEHAVIOR* BY DONALD SNYGG AND
ARTHUR COMBS, PUBLISHED BY HARPER AND BROTHERS
IN 1949

p. 14   This does not rule out the
         importance of past humans

p. 34   also appli-
         cable to ph.
         field which
         is a figure
         of speech

p. 37   will this partly
         explain forgetting

p. 138   adequate phen. self

         assuming
         she, is okay

TRANSCRIPTION OF MARGINALIA FOUND IN A DIFFERENT
LIBRARY COPY OF *INDIVIDUAL BEHAVIOR* BY DONALD
SNYGG AND ARTHUR COMBS, PUBLISHED BY HARPER AND
BROTHERS IN 1949

p. 6   ✔

p. 8   ✔

        ✔

p. 12   ✔

        ✔

        ✔

p. 15   def

p. 45   review

p. 48   instinct

p. 67   def
        note

p. 111 threat uppermost

p. 317 should come
        perceive

"self"

'internal
reality'

relation of 2

p. 345 the
coward
the
sentimentalist

COMPLETE TRANSCRIPTION OF PENNED MARGINALIA
FOUND IN A LIBRARY COPY OF CARL JASPERS'
NIETZSCHE & CHRISTIANITY PUBLISHED IN 1961 BY
HENRY REGNERY COMPANY

p. viii   **CORE**

p. 7   **N.**

p. 17   **Bliss**

p. 76   **Attack
on
Science**

p. 100   **illness**

p. 8   Overtly simplifying

        as in
        dreams

    Fantastic
    sequence of haphazardly
    associative imagery

p. 23   Also

    structure!

p. 40   prevents
    dullness

p. 54   in something or someone:
    quality arousing feelings of
    pity, sympathy and tenderness
    or sorrow in another

p. 55   keeping silent

p. 82   But

p. 97   Distance effect by "Time"
    past

p. 131   introspection, self-
          examination

p. 287   love
          &
          discovery